Bitcoin

----- ❦❧ -----

How to go from Beginner to Pro in Bitcoin

Bowen Bloggsbot

© **Copyright 2016 by Bowen Bloggsbot**
- All rights reserved.

The follow eBook is reproduced below with the goal of providing information that is as accurate and reliable as possible. Regardless, purchasing this eBook can be seen as consent to the fact that both the publisher and the author of this book are in no way experts on the topics discussed within and that any recommendations or suggestions that are made herein are for entertainment purposes only. Professionals should be consulted as needed prior to undertaking any of the action endorsed herein.

This declaration is deemed fair and valid by both the American Bar Association and the Committee of Publishers Association and is legally binding throughout the United States.

Furthermore, the transmission, duplication or reproduction of any of the following work including specific information will be considered an illegal act irrespective of if it is done electronically or in print. This extends to creating a secondary or tertiary copy of the work or a recorded copy and is only allowed with express written consent from the Publisher. All additional right reserved.

The information in the following pages is broadly considered to be a truthful and accurate account of facts and as such any inattention, use or misuse of the information in question by the reader will render any resulting actions solely under their purview. There are no scenarios in which the publisher or the original author of this work can be in any fashion deemed liable for any hardship or damages that may befall them after undertaking information described herein.

Additionally, the information in the following pages is intended only for informational purposes and should thus be thought of as universal. As befitting its nature, it is presented without assurance regarding its prolonged validity or interim quality. Trademarks that are mentioned are done without written consent and can in no way be considered an endorsement from the trademark holder.

Table of Contents

Introduction 1

Chapter 1: An Introduction to Bitcoin 3

Chapter 2: Cryptocurrency Technologies 11

Chapter 3: Bitcoin Mining 17

Chapter 4: Investing and Trading in Bitcoins . 27

Chapter 5: The Blockchain 43

Chapter 6: Bitcoin Wallet 57

Conclusion 63

Introduction

Congratulations on downloading this book and thank you for doing so.

The following chapters will discuss everything you need to know about Bitcoins. Up until 2013, few people were aware of or interested in Bitcoin. Today, there is so much interest in this digital currency that it is important to learn more about it.

In this book, we will discuss everything you need to know about Bitcoin. We will define Bitcoin and take a look at this digital currency. We will also look at the cryptocurrency technology that has made Bitcoin such a successful and rewarding currency.

This book will also teach you how to buy Bitcoins, where to find them, where to store them and even how to trade and invest in them. You will learn what a Bitcoin wallet is and why you need one. Digital wallets need to be kept

Bitcoin

very secure and you will learn just how to keep your Bitcoin wallet secure so that your money remains safe at all times.

We believe that knowledge is power and you need this knowledge in order to empower yourself before investing in Bitcoins. Therefore, read this book and learn as much as you can about Bitcoins. This way, you will be empowered enough to venture into the world of Bitcoins and all the exciting rewards it has to offer.

There are plenty of books on this subject on the market, thanks again for choosing this one! Every effort was made to ensure it is full of as much useful information as possible, please enjoy!

Chapter 1:

An Introduction to Bitcoin

Bitcoin definition

Bitcoin is a digital currency and also a digital payment system. It is widely used all over the world as a cryptocurrency and is accepted as a means of exchange, in trade, investment, and savings.

Bitcoin was invented by someone by the alias Satoshi Nakamoto in 2009. His real name is not known. Some suspect it was created by a group of programmers by the same pseudo name. However, this currency has gained worldwide acceptance and is very popular due to its many benefits.

Bitcoin is a decentralized currency. This means that it is not regulated by any authority. There is no Central Bank or Reserve Bank anywhere in the world that regulates this cryptocurrency.

Peer-to-peer system

Bitcoin was released as an open-source software and operates a peer-to-peer system. This means all computers are connected to each other at the same level without a main server or administrator. This system enables everyone to view all transactions, which helps maintain the integrity of the system.

Fees and charges

Most regular payment platforms such as PayPal, credit cards and all others that use regular currencies often charge very high fees. Sometimes payments take days to go through, especially when sending money overseas.

Bitcoin is completely different. There are minimal fees charged for transfer, exchange or other transactions. This is one of the most attractive features of Bitcoin. Another feature is that Bitcoin payments are almost instantaneous regardless of where a transaction is conducted.

This means someone in the US can pay a person in Asia or Africa and the payment reflects in the

Chapter 1: An Introduction to Bitcoin

system shortly thereafter. Compare this to international wire transfers which take approximately 3 days to clear. These are some of the reasons that make Bitcoin so popular and a preferred currency.

Using Bitcoins

You can use Bitcoins for all kinds of transactions. For instance, you can buy goods, pay for services and even send to friends and family anywhere in the world. There are many businesses that accept Bitcoins for payment. They include hotels, restaurants, retail stores, grocery stores, flower shops and many others.

Popular stores that accept Bitcoins include Microsoft, Amazon, eBay, Shopify, Dell and many others. Bitcoin is a popular online currency and is currently the most widely used cryptocurrency in the world.

Bitcoin valuation

Bitcoin is not regulated by any government. Therefore, its value strictly depends on market forces. This means it depends on demand and supply. Now since supply is limited and demand keeps increasing, the value of Bitcoin has risen astronomically in the last 5 years.

Bitcoin

Bitcoin is generally overseen by its huge network and community. You can buy Bitcoin just like you can any other currency. However, you will need to go to an exchange. At the exchange, you will be able to buy Bitcoin using other currencies such as dollars, pounds, euros, and others.

Once you purchase Bitcoins, they will be stored in your digital wallet. Before you actually invest in Bitcoins, you should open a wallet and ensure that it is very secure. This is because Bitcoin is a digital currency that can be compromised.

Bitcoin uses decentralized technology to enable secure payments and for the storage of money that requires no banking services or people's names. There is a reason why people around the world love Bitcoin. One is that they find value in a currency that is not exposed to bank charges and free of government control.

Bitcoin is also popular because it is seen as a currency that provides anonymity and privacy. However, it is sometimes the preferred currency of choice by people who deal in contraband.

Over the years, the value of Bitcoin has increased phenomenally. As of March 2017, 1 Bitcoin was worth $1268. By September 2017, the value had

Chapter 1: An Introduction to Bitcoin

risen to $3700. A person who invested $1000 in Bitcoin in 2010 is worth $37 million today. That is how much this currency has grown in that time.

How Bitcoin works

As per its definition, Bitcoin is a virtual currency that runs on the Blockchain. The blockchain is a powerful, decentralized ledger that records all Bitcoin transactions in real time. All transactions are updated regularly and records are accessible and can be viewed by all network users.

Bitcoins are mined by Bitcoin miners. Bitcoin mining is the process by which new Bitcoins come into existence. The process of mining is quite technical. It requires powerful computers that run on special software. The miners basically have to solve a complex puzzle. If they are successful then they get rewarded for their efforts.

There is a maximum number of Bitcoins that can come into existence. The system is designed to allow a maximum of only 21 million Bitcoins. Once this limit is achieved by the Bitcoin miners, there will be no more to add to the system.

Bitcoin

Currently, there are about 25 million BTC in circulation.

What factors affect the value of Bitcoin?

There are a number of factors that do play a major role in determining the value of Bitcoin. The biggest of them all is demand. As demand keeps rising and supply grows slowly, the value keeps increasing dramatically.

When one of the largest online Bitcoin exchanges collapsed in 2013, the price of Bitcoin tumbled. Mt Gox was the largest Bitcoin exchange in the world. Upon its collapse, the value of Bitcoin came crashing. It has since been rising steadily over the years.

Signs that regulators are slowly warming up to Bitcoin and other cryptocurrencies have also helped boost confidence in these currencies. When more and more people feel confident trading and using Bitcoins, then its value definitely goes up.

There are currently about 5.8 million people who have cryptocurrency wallets and use Bitcoin. These people are located in the USA, Canada, Europe and other countries from around the world.

Chapter 1: An Introduction to Bitcoin

These Bitcoin holders use it for various, different purposes. Popular use includes making investments where fees and charges do not apply, funding businesses and companies and in online trades.

There are many online stores and outlets that accept Bitcoin and approve its use as a means of digital payment. There are cash outlets that accept Bitcoins. In some countries, you can convert your Bitcoins into cash. Even brick and mortar establishments accept Bitcoin payments. For instance, you have Your Sushi restaurant, Dell Computers, CEX stores and others.

Is it Bitcoin safe?

Bitcoin is a very safe currency. However, you have to take very strong precautions if you buy, purchase or otherwise trade in this cryptocurrency. The reason is, while Bitcoin is encrypted, it can be stolen by hackers. Many people and organizations have lost colossal amounts when their Bitcoins were stolen through hacking.

Therefore, if you get a Bitcoin wallet, ensure that it is encrypted and protected with a strong password. A good password to use with

Bitcoin

cryptocurrencies is one that contains upper and lowercase letters, numbers and non-alphanumeric characters.

When you purchase Bitcoins, you will receive them in digital format. You should store them in your wallet and, if you can, store the wallet offline. This way, your Bitcoins will remain safe. Sometimes hackers get into the system and steal their Bitcoins.

People are wondering whether they should invest in Bitcoin. There are those who chose to invest in this cryptocurrency a few years back. Many of them were rewarded handsomely. However, Bitcoin is a very volatile currency. This volatility can work for or against an investor. Therefore, think carefully and consider all your options before investing.

Bitcoins do not exist in a physical manner. Since Bitcoin is a digital currency, balances are maintained on public ledgers within the Bitcoin cloud known as Blockchain. Currently, there are no banks issuing or accepting Bitcoins. Even then, Bitcoin remains quite popular with consumers and traders. Its value has been increasing rapidly though it remains quite volatile.

Chapter 2:

Cryptocurrency Technologies

An introduction to cryptocurrencies

Cryptocurrency simply means a digital media of exchange that uses cryptography. In cryptocurrency technology, cryptography is essential to secure the transactions and to control the creation of additional units of the currency.

Cryptocurrencies such as Bitcoin are considered a subset of digital currencies. Digital currencies are electronic currencies that do not exist in physical forms such as bank notes or coins. However, they are widely used to make payments and accepted as a currency. They include cryptocurrencies and virtual currencies.

While most digital currencies are used within a given community, only Bitcoin has gained worldwide recognition. It is the most popular of all cryptocurrencies. There are other cryptocurrencies in circulation as well. They are mostly referred to as altcoins, short for alternative coins.

Decentralization of cryptocurrency

Bitcoin is the first decentralized cryptocurrency. This means there is no central body that administers or controls Bitcoin. The same is true for all other decentralized currencies. Instead, the control is managed through something known as the Blockchain. Other cryptocurrencies in circulation include NameCoin, LiteCoin, and PPCoin.

Bitcoin is transacted on a platform known as Blockchain. Blockchain ensures that all Bitcoin transactions are secure, private and recorded. Records of a transaction can clearly be viewed on the Blockchain shortly after a transaction takes place. All active Bitcoin users have access to Blockchain and will be able to view any transaction they choose to.

The Bitcoin Blockchain is a public ledger of the transactions that occur within the system. Blockchain also makes use of a Timestamp. This

Chapter 2: Cryptocurrency Technologies

ensures that the ledger records are well maintained and can be confirmed. Transactions can also be traced back to the very first one within the Blockchain.

Breaking down cryptocurrencies

Since cryptocurrencies are private and anonymous, some people take advantage of this and use them for illicit purposes. For instance, people have been known to use cryptocurrencies for tax evasion and money laundering.

Currently, there are over 14.6 million Bitcoins in circulation with a market value of over $3.4 billion. This number is capped at about 21 million Bitcoins. Once that number is achieved, no more Bitcoins will be generated.

Now since cryptocurrencies are digital and have no regulatory authority or central depository, they can be compromised. A digital balance can easily be deleted and even wiped out should a computer crash. It is advisable to backup data to prevent a major loss.

If you have plenty of Bitcoins worth a lot of money, then you should not hold them all in one wallet. Spread them out in order to minimize the risk. This is akin to putting all your money in one wallet then going out.

Despite all these, cryptocurrencies are considered safe and can preserve value and are easier to transport. They are not as expensive to handle compared to cash and transactions cost much less. Users also love them because they are out of reach of central bank authorities and also facilitate exchange.

These currencies are not immune to hacking. This is why it is important to split your money and store it in separate wallets. For added security, you should use complex passwords, 2-layer security and even store your digital wallet offline.

The pros and cons of cryptocurrencies

Cryptocurrencies have both benefits and drawbacks. Most people wish to know what the pros and cons are before they consider investing in or using cryptocurrencies.

Pros

Cryptocurrencies have simplified the process of sending currency from one person or business to another. Transactions occur in real time,

Chapter 2: Cryptocurrency Technologies

regardless of where the sender and receiver are located.

Cryptocurrencies also provide convenience and anonymity when transacting. While the transaction is recorded and then entered into the ledger, privacy and anonymity are maintained.

The costs of transactions are minimal and almost non-existent. This is because transactions are free between parties. This means that transactions are not just very fast even across continents but almost free.

Cons

Cryptocurrencies face a couple of challenges. One of these is volatility. For instance, Bitcoin is a very volatile currency. It gains a lot of value in a short period of time then loses most of it. This puts users at risk of incurring losses.

Cryptocurrency transactions are anonymous in nature. Transactions usually cannot be traced back to individuals or companies. This makes the systems vulnerable to abuse by criminals.

These currencies are often at risk of being hacked. While the system is pretty safe,

Bitcoin

individual users can have their wallets or computers hacked and cryptocurrencies stolen.

Chapter 3:

Bitcoin Mining

Most people are unaware of how Bitcoins come into existence. Bitcoin is a cryptocurrency used to transact online. However, where do Bitcoins come from? The answer is simple. Bitcoins are mined.

What is Bitcoin mining?

In broader terms, Bitcoin mining can be defined as the process through which all Bitcoin transactions are carried out, verified and then entered into the public ledger known as Blockchain.

But in much simpler terms, the phrase Bitcoin mining can be described as a process that uses computers to solve complex mathematical puzzles. Therefore, for any single Bitcoin to come into existence and get into the system, it has to be mined.

The Bitcoin mining process is meant to be challenging in order to limit the number of Bitcoins added to the system on a regular basis. This way, the system remains stable and users maintain their confidence.

Bitcoin mining process

The Bitcoin mining process actually achieves two purposes. The first one is the generation of new Bitcoins into existence while the other ensures that all recent Bitcoin transactions are accurately added to the Blockchain.

The process of Bitcoin mining is decentralized. This basically means the process does not have to take place at one central location but from any location. Therefore, anyone with the right equipment can actually generate Bitcoins and add them to the system.

The challenges of the mining process

For the Bitcoin system to remain secure, then the mining process has to be decentralized and remain that way. In order to mine Bitcoins, you

Chapter 3: Bitcoin Mining

will need a powerful computer that can handle the tough computer puzzles it has to solve.

Bitcoin mining can be challenging depending on the effort put in the process. As more Bitcoins are added to the system, the challenge of creating new ones becomes even more challenging. This is automatically adjusted by the system about every two weeks.

Mining rewards

Those who mine Bitcoins do so for a reward. The mining releases Bitcoins in blocks. For each block mined comes a new Bitcoin. And the reward for mining the block is a block reward. Currently, the reward for mining one block is 25 Bitcoins. Prior to that, it was 50 Bitcoins.

In total, there can only be 21 million Bitcoins in circulation. Once this number is achieved, no more Bitcoins will be mined. Block rewards are the main incentive for miners. This reward is currently at 0.3% of the mining revenue. So, if 50 Bitcoins are released per block, then the miners receive 0.3% of 50 Bitcoins.

Bitcoin mining

There are normally a number of Bitcoin miners in operation at any given time. Now, these miners are not at one specific location but could be anywhere in the world. What is important is that they are connected to the blockchain and follow laid down protocol.

The Bitcoin miner who solves the computational puzzle first gets to enjoy the reward. The miner also gets to add the block into the blockchain network. But as the block diminishes, the incentive also diminishes and miners become less incentivized to continue with the mining process.

Mining difficulties

Bitcoin mining is not as simple as it sounds. However, the level of difficulty will depend on a couple of factors. These include the software in use, the power of the computer and the cost of electricity or power.

The Bitcoin mining difficulty level is adjusted after every 2016 blocks. This means that after every two weeks. The aim of the adjustment is to stabilize the block discovery process and number of Bitcoins released. Thus, as more Bitcoins are

Chapter 3: Bitcoin Mining

released into the Blockchain, the computational puzzles keep getting more complicated. This then creates the need for faster and more powerful computers.

Common Bitcoin mining hardware

If you wish to mine Bitcoins and add them to the blockchain, then there is certain equipment that you will require. Initially, the miners used regular desktop computers with a regular CPU. However, these are not as powerful as required. They moved to GPU or graphics processing units which are more powerful and performed much better.

However, in today's world, the computing world is so competitive. To mine Bitcoins efficiently, you will need the latest ASIC computer. The term ASIC stands for Application Specific Integrated Circuit. In today's world, Bitcoin mining has become so competitive that only those with the latest ASICs computers can do so profitably. Without the latest model, it becomes more expensive to mine Bitcoins compared to the reward.

Now the power and sophistication of the latest ASICS computer has increased over the years.

This means that computational puzzles are solved faster as there is more power available. However, this also leads to an increase in the complexity of the puzzles. The reason why people are investing heavily in Bitcoin mining is due to the rewards offered and the rapid increase in the Bitcoin price.

Formation of mining pools

Now since the costs of mining have increased rapidly over the years, it becomes difficult for individual miners to remain profitable. Those with very little mining power can team up with other miners experiencing the same problem and then put their resources together.

Take for instance a miner with a small percentage of mining power. Such a miner has very little chance of discovering a Bitcoin block on their own. There are investments required, such as purchasing of a mining card. This card alone costs $1000 yet it only has 0.001% of the mining power held by the network. Such a miner runs the risk of losing out completely even as they invest in electricity and a good quality ASICs computer costing over $2400.

Chapter 3: Bitcoin Mining

It would be easier for such a miner to team up with other miners and pool their resources together. There are mining pools that are managed by Third Parties. These are coordinated by groups of miners who get together to achieve what they are not able to achieve individually.

Miners who pool resources together are able to achieve more together and solve Bitcoin computer puzzles faster. They will then receive more rewards which are then shared equitably among pool members. This means miners receive rewards according to the inputs they made.

Energy costs associated with Bitcoin mining

Another factor that is very important is the energy cost associated with Bitcoin mining. All mining operations use huge amounts of electricity. They do need reliable electricity supply as well as cooling systems.

Many mining operations are located very close to energy sources. One of the largest Bitcoin mining companies in the US, managed by Mega-Big-Power, is located along the Columbia River in

Washington. In this state, electricity is in abundant supply and is very cheap.

Another company, Cloud-Hashing, undertakes Bitcoin mining operations in Iceland. The electricity generated here is very affordable and the cool temperature helps to cool down the computer systems. When considering putting up Bitcoin mining operations, then this is an important factor to consider.

Bitcoin mining and regulation

Sometime back, the IRS provided some guidelines regarding Bitcoin. The guidelines indicated that Bitcoin miners could be considered as self-employed individuals and as such are liable to pay tax.

However, according to the same body, Bitcoin miners are not considered as money transmitters and can therefore not be taxed as such. Similarly, firms providing cloud mining services are not considered as money transmitters.

In summary

New Bitcoins come into circulation through a process known as Bitcoin mining. The total number of Bitcoins that will ever be in

Chapter 3: Bitcoin Mining

circulation is capped at 21 million. Those who engage in the production of Bitcoins are referred to as miners. They need special equipment and software to produce Bitcoins.

Chapter 4:

Investing and Trading in Bitcoins

There has been a remarkable interest shown in Bitcoin in recent days. While Bitcoin has been around since 2009, it has recently captured the attention of investors due to its phenomenal growth in value.

For instance, since its inception till 2012, it gained over 300% in value and from 2013 to 2015, its value increased further by 400%. This kind of growth is definitely going to attract the right kind of attention.

Investing in Bitcoin

Putting your money in Bitcoin is very different from investing in stocks and securities. Investing in Bitcoins varies in two distinct ways from investing your money in the stock exchange.

Bitcoin

1. Bitcoin is a very volatile currency

One outstanding factor about Bitcoin is that it is very volatile. This means that its value changes drastically and frequently. This volatility is quite unpredictable. Investors therefore need to be very wary of this volatility as it could easily wipe off their investments or make them fabulously wealthy.

2. The securities market loves Bitcoin

Plenty of traders, fund managers, and investment clubs love Bitcoin. These investors have invested in Bitcoin and have made it part of their portfolio. Stock market traders are used to volatility and know how to approach volatile investments.

Basics of Bitcoin and cryptocurrency investments

Now Bitcoin is a popular decentralized cryptocurrency system that is accessible from anywhere in the world. It operates on software that was released in 2009 and continues to be improved by a network of developers. These developers are funded by the Bitcoin Foundation.

Chapter 4: Investing and Trading in Bitcoins

Bitcoin became attractive to investors from 2013 after registering phenomenal growth and gaining value drastically. Recent performance has been exciting but volatile. However, stock market investors are used to volatility and are able to take care of this eventuality.

Venture capital firms were among the first serious investors in Bitcoin. Within the first 6 months of 2014, they put in more than $130 million in this volatile cryptocurrency. In the previous year, 2012, they had put in almost $90 million in Bitcoin. Thus, they almost doubled their investments. Prior to that Bitcoin was barely able to generate $2.2 million from investors. Today, September 2017, Bitcoin continues to grow and demand keeps rising from hungry investors seeking a share of the profits that Bitcoin generates.

How to invest in Bitcoin as an ordinary person

One of the easiest ways for any regular person to invest in Bitcoin is to simply buy some. There are lots of online Bitcoin exchanges where anyone with some money can buy some Bitcoins. Residents of the USA can buy Bitcoins from the popular Bitcoin exchange, CoinBase. CoinBase

Bitcoin continues to be a popular platform for investors who wish to invest or buy Bitcoins. They sell Bitcoins at a rate of 1% above prevailing market rates.

For residents of the US who wish to use CoinBase to buy Bitcoins, there are options available to invest in Bitcoin. For instance, they can link their bank accounts with their personal CoinBase wallets and buy Bitcoins directly. Alternatively, they can use other payment methods such as the use of credit cards and online payment platforms such as PayPal.

It is important to remember that CoinBase is not an exchange. Investors who use their services will simply be buying Bitcoins from sellers through the firm. CoinBase offers the option of automatic buying. For instance, you can set up the system to buy you $50 worth of Bitcoins each month. You can also do this on a weekly or fortnightly basis. However, automatic buy does not allow you to determine the price at which you buy Bitcoins so it is important to be wary.

As a small-scale investor, you can buy Bitcoins slowly over a period of time and keep them until the price increases significantly. Now, if you prefer to buy from a Bitcoin exchange in the US,

Chapter 4: Investing and Trading in Bitcoins

then you can check out one of the more popular exchanges such as BitStamp. At this Bitcoin exchange, you stand to get a better deal because you will deal directly with other Bitcoin holders, especially sellers. You will, therefore, not have to pay any commissions, fees or charges.

At the Bitcoin exchanges, liquidity is quite high so it very possible to find sellers offering Bitcoins and you can also convert any Bitcoins you have into dollars. There is a small fee charged by the exchange which is ranges from 0.5% down to 0.2%. The rate will depend on the amounts you are trading with larger amounts attracting lower rates.

Other options of buying Bitcoins as an individual investor

Apart from CoinBase and the Bitcoin exchanges, you can also find Bitcoins on offer at Local Bitcoin, an online company at the URL address www.Bitcoin.com. This online Bitcoin platform brings together Bitcoin buyers and sellers and provides them with tools and a platform where they can deal conveniently.

At the moment, Bitcoin is quite popular with many investors expressing an interest in this global cryptocurrency. However, volatility still remains the biggest challenge. This means that most buyers simply buy into Bitcoin and sell at the earliest opportunity. Volatility would reduce drastically if some of the larger investors held onto their Bitcoins a little longer.

Check out all these Bitcoin platforms before you decide which one to settle on. Each of them has advantages and disadvantages so choose carefully. Also, consider the volatile nature of Bitcoin when investing.

Investing in cryptocurrencies like Bitcoins

Cryptocurrencies have now become popular in most investment portfolios. Lots of large investors such as retirement schemes, investment funds, and pension funds have cryptocurrencies such as Bitcoin. This is because of the long-term potential as well as the good returns enjoyed in recent years.

Cryptocurrencies are unregulated, decentralized and not controlled by any government entity. And while they are digital or virtual in nature, they can be exchanged for regular currency such as dollars and pounds. This means that

Chapter 4: Investing and Trading in Bitcoins

cryptocurrencies operate, for the most part just like regular fiat currencies.

The major difference between such currencies and ordinary currencies is that cryptocurrencies cannot be converted into physical cash or cold money. A single Bitcoin cannot exist physically the way a dollar bill would. This may pose some challenges when it comes to trading with Bitcoins and other cryptocurrencies.

Investment opportunities with Bitcoin

Investors have for some time now viewed cryptocurrencies as providing a speculative investment opportunity. This means that while the cryptocurrencies are volatile in nature, they will eventually stabilize at higher prices at a later date and this offers a chance to earn a profit.

One of the best ways of investing in Bitcoins and other cryptocurrencies is to buy a certain quantity from an exchange, hold it for a while, wait until the prices fluctuate upwards to a significant level and then sell them for other hard currencies such as the dollar.

This strategy has been tried and proven to work. A lot of people in the USA and around the world are investing in Bitcoins in this way. It is possible to open an account with an exchange, buy Bitcoins and store them in your Bitcoin wallet, then hold onto them until there is a price increase then go ahead and sell at the same exchange. You can then convert your gains into hard currency such as the dollar.

Combating the volatility of Bitcoin and other cryptocurrencies

Bitcoin has in recent years emerged as a new asset class and lucrative investment option for investors from all over the world. This is largely due to its excellent ability to overcome cross-border exchanges, the capacity to store value, diversify an investment portfolio and as a medium of exchange.

As an example, the IRS has approved the Bitcoin IRA which is a retirement account based on the Bitcoin. This IRA allows for the addition of Bitcoins into the retirement portfolio. Others that have added Bitcoin as part of their portfolio include ARK Investment Management's EFT, GBTC or Grayscale Bitcoin Investment Trust and others, all which trade with Bitcoins.

Chapter 4: Investing and Trading in Bitcoins

Volatility of Bitcoin

One of the most popular ways that investors can combat Bitcoin volatility is through the use of the SIP or Systematic Investment Plan. This plan is largely based on a popular investment technique known as dollar-cost averaging.

Combating the volatility

Now, to combat this inherent volatility, Bitcoins should be strategically purchased. Instead of going to an exchange and spending a large amount on Bitcoins, it is advisable to purchase smaller, fixed amounts on a regular basis.

This simply means buying a certain small number of Bitcoins periodically. This is one way of combating volatility. They should buy, for instance, $500 each week, regardless of the price. This helps stabilize the currency and keep it from dramatic rise and fall of value. This also ensures that investors who follow this path will be able to get the most out of it. The benefits of this kind of approach include:

- Inculcating discipline in Bitcoin trading

- It helps reduce the concerns about the best time to purchase an asset

Bitcoin

- The average cost of Bitcoins will come down due to this approach
- Investors will have the convenience and less commitment regarding money spent

Example

Consider an investor who purchased Bitcoins regularly in 2012. In this year, the lowest Bitcoin price was approximately $4.20 and the highest price $13.70. a regular buyer who invested in Bitcoins consistently throughout the year would have paid an average price of $7.75 in that year. Such a trend helps stabilize the price and reduce the currency's volatility.

In fact, analysts claim that the volatility would reduce further if they held onto their Bitcoins for longer. Volatility results largely due to investors offloading their Bitcoins almost as soon as there is a price variance, usually within a matter of days or weeks.

In the USA, one of the best ways of benefit from long-term Bitcoin investment includes investment in Roth IRA offered through the Bitcoin IRA. This type of Roth is known as the SIPBIT. This kind of investment is regarded as

Chapter 4: Investing and Trading in Bitcoins

one of the most convenient and tax-efficient ways of long-term investment in Bitcoins.

Therefore, the best and smartest way to invest in Bitcoin today is investing smaller amounts and then holding onto the cryptocurrency. This way, as an investor, you will be able to withstand the drastic price changes and also have an additional asset class within your portfolio basket.

Also, remember to purchase Bitcoins at regular intervals and then hold. This provides you with convenience, flexibility and much better returns, especially in the long term. You will also significantly lower your risk.

Bitcoin investment concerns

As an investor, you need to be aware of the risks associated with Bitcoin investments. Experts still maintain that Bitcoin is a largely speculative investment with plenty of vulnerabilities.

Hackers have, in the last couple of years, gained access to people's digital wallets. Just last year, 2016, hackers stole more than $50 million worth of cryptocurrencies from investors in the investment fund DAO.

Bitcoin

The volatile nature of cryptocurrencies cannot be ignored, especially for short-term investors. Prices sometimes fall greatly but also rise dramatically. If you are an investor in Bitcoins, then you are best advised to hold your position, especially after a dramatic event.

Trading in Bitcoins

One of the more popular ways of making money today is trading in Bitcoins. Investors consider Bitcoin cryptocurrency as a high risk, high reward asset. No one has any idea how high it will rise on one day or how low it will fall the next.

Bitcoins are popular across the globe and it is this that makes this cryptocurrency such an attractive investment tool. It can be seamlessly traded across borders and transactions approved instantly. While rewards are very attractive, short-term risks are high as well. Caution should, therefore, be taken and risks calculated wisely.

Process of trading in Bitcoins

Bitcoin is virtual currency but it is a currency nevertheless, just like the dollar, pound or yen. The only major difference is that it does not exist

Chapter 4: Investing and Trading in Bitcoins

in a tangible form. However, you can buy it, sell it, use it as an investment tool and trade with it.

To trade using Bitcoins, you simply need to use your dollars to buy Bitcoins, wait until an opportune time then sell them and convert your earnings back to dollars. This is the strategy that most small-scale, short-term investors adopt. They stand a chance to make some money but they may incur losses in the process to ensure that you trade only with money that you can afford to lose.

What you will need to trade effectively is an account with one of these exchanges. You want to buy and sell at an exchange because you encounter other buyers and sellers directly. Using non-exchange platforms only delays your trades while costing you money in fees and charges.

The Bitcoin exchange

The Bitcoin exchange is an exchange almost similar to a currency or stock market exchange. Traders visit the Bitcoin exchange simply to purchase or sell Bitcoins. Most Bitcoin exchanges allow multiple international currencies such as dollars, yen, pounds and the euro. This is because Bitcoin is international and is traded by traders from all around the world.

At the exchange, Bitcoin is treated just like a commodity such as oil, silver, steel and so on. Most of the time, Bitcoins are exchanged for dollars and then the dollars are converted into other currencies. This is because Bitcoin is mostly denominated in the dollar rather than in other international currencies.

Trade Bitcoins directly at the exchange

One of the best ways of making money on the exchange is to trade Bitcoins directly. As an investor or trader, arm yourself with dollars from your bank and proceed to buy Bitcoins at the prevailing market rates. At the Bitcoin exchange, you will be charged a nominal fee, usually just 1% of your trade.

Once you purchase the Bitcoins, they will be transferred to your online digital wallet. You will need a Bitcoin wallet if you are to buy, sell or deal in Bitcoins. A wallet is essential so you should have one. Ensure that it is as secure as possible otherwise hackers may attempt to fraudulently gain access.

Chapter 4: Investing and Trading in Bitcoins

Find a trustworthy Bitcoin broker

Instead of trading directly at the Bitcoin exchange, you may choose to use the services of a trusted broker. A broker is one who can place trades and buy and sell Bitcoins on your behalf. The aim is that he makes you some money or earns you a good profit. Using a broker has its advantages. For instance, the broker will keep a watch on the markets for you. Therefore, you will not need to check markets each day to note the performance. This saves you time, protects you from drastic losses and market volatility and ensures you earn a profit from the trades.

Bitcoin trading process

First, you need to identify a trustworthy Bitcoin exchange and open an account.

Get yourself a Bitcoin wallet. Ensure that it is secure with various security features.

Connect your account with a payment system and then transfer funds to your Bitcoin exchange account.

Now you may purchase a number of Bitcoins you want at your preferred price.

Bitcoin

Once you buy the Bitcoins, put them in your Bitcoin wallet and then keep it safe.

Find the strategies that suit you the most and maximize on these strategies to earn you a profit while avoiding losses.

Points to keep in mind

Trading in Bitcoins is relatively easy and straightforward but remember Bitcoin is very volatile and you risk losing your all your money.

Ensure that you have a very secure wallet and, if you can, store your wallet offline. Only get it online when you wish to trade or exchange your Bitcoins.

Also, make sure that you revamp your computer's security. You should have sufficient protection against malware and viruses. Update your antivirus software regularly and ensure your firewalls function appropriately.

Chapter 5:

The Blockchain

The blockchain, in reference to Bitcoins, is the public ledger of all Bitcoin transactions that take place. It is essentially a public record that shows all transactions when users buy, sell, or trade their Bitcoins.

The blockchain also lets users know when new Bitcoins are mined and added to the ledger. It is always growing as new blocks are added to it on a regular basis. When Bitcoin miners are mining to generate new Bitcoins, they do so in blocks. A single block may cause the release of about 25 Bitcoins.

Bitcoin blocks

These new blocks are regularly added to the Bitcoin blockchain in a chronological and linear order. The blockchain consists of computers that are interconnected to each other. Each computer that is connected to the Bitcoin network is referred to as a node.

Each Bitcoin node in the network with a client who executes the task of validating and relaying all Bitcoin transactions will receive a copy of the updated blockchain. This copy is normally downloaded automatically upon joining the network. Therefore, users are able to view each and every transaction.

Understanding the blockchain

One of the greatest technologies to emerge from Bitcoin is definitely the blockchain. It is the main innovation and the backbone of the Bitcoin system. The Bitcoin blockchain is the network that records all transactions and is proof about all the transactions that have ever taken place.

The blockchain consists of blocks which are a series of records of recent transactions. A single block on the network is simply a record of some or all of the recent transactions. Once a single block is updated and completed, it is added to the blockchain and becomes available to anyone who wishes to confirm a transaction.

Chapter 5: The Blockchain

As soon as one block is completed and added to the network, a new one is generated. Therefore, there are a countless number of blocks in the blockchain. These blocks are not randomly added to the blockchain but are linked together just like a chain in an organized, linear and chronological manner. Each block will always have the hash of the preceding block.

Blockchain and bank records

The blockchain can be reliably compared to banking transactions. For each bank account, there exists a ledger of all transactions such as cash deposits, check deposits, withdrawals and so on. These entries are usually entered in the manner or order in which they occur.

In this analogy, the block serves as an account or individual bank statement. The only difference is the privacy of bank transactions. When it comes to Bitcoin blockchain, the ledgers are available to anyone within the Bitcoin network connected via a node.

Blockchain protocol

As a matter of protocol, the blockchain information is accessible by all nodes that are currently accessing the system. The information is held in a database but is updated periodically.

In fact, the entire copy of the blockchain contains the record of each and every Bitcoin that has ever been transacted. Using the blockchain, therefore, it is possible to get insights into facts such as the value of transactions relating to a given address.

There are some who consider the ever-growing blockchain to be a growing problem as it presents challenges when it comes to synchronization and storage. Basically, there is an extra block added to the Bitcoin blockchain every 10 minutes. These are often generated through Bitcoin mining processes.

Blockchain is a distributed database

It is possible to view the blockchain as one single spreadsheet which is then duplicated numerous numbers of times over a large computer network that spreads around the world. It is then accurately and regularly updated so that record is available to any interested person within the network.

Blockchain technology is used mostly with Bitcoins. In recent times though, it has found use in many different areas, mostly those in the

Chapter 5: The Blockchain

financial services sector. Firms and organizations such as banks are looking favorably at this technology and how it can provide its numerous benefits, such as security, real-time updates of ledger entries and so on. There are a number of institutions that have currently updated the blockchain to suit their own operations.

The data contained on the blockchain is never held centrally. The information held therein is distributed and is instantly available to any user within the network of computers connected together. This makes it very difficult for hackers and other unauthorized users who may wish to compromise the system and make unauthorized access. This makes it a safe, secure and reliable system.

Google docs and the blockchain

It is easy to view the blockchain as a Google document. First, think about sharing a Word article with someone else such as a friend. Your friend is able to make changes to the Word document but you will not be able to see these changes unless or until they send the document back to you. This is essentially how current databases work.

Bitcoin

Compare this to Google docs. In this situation, you and your sender or receiver can simultaneously view the document, view edits and changes in real time and so on. This kind of technology is what is available on the blockchain.

As Bitcoin users transact, the transactions are available instantly and can be viewed by every member of the network all at the same time. This is a great application that you can find useful, not just with Bitcoin transactions but with many others too. Think about mortgages, banking or finance, and even the stock market.

Blockchain is very robust and durable

It is also right to compare the blockchain to a reliable Internet. Now blockchain stores its information all across the entire network. This means it is not centrally controlled and therefore the possibility of failure at any node is non-existent.

Bitcoin was invented back in 2008 and made available from 2009. Since its inception, it has used the blockchain technology yet it has never faced any major or serious challenges in its operations.

Chapter 5: The Blockchain

A lot of the challenges or disruptions that the Bitcoin blockchain has suffered are only administrative and due to hacking. In the same way, the Internet has been in existence for about 30 odd years yet it has been rather durable and successful in that period of time. It has a splendid track record of success and Bitcoin is following fast in this trend.

The Bitcoin blockchain is transparent and incorruptible

One of the most outstanding features of the blockchain is that it is a very transparent ledger system. Unlike banks and other financial institutions which have very secretive operations and procedures, the blockchain has been totally transparent and all transactions are in the open.

Blockchain is incorruptible

The Bitcoin blockchain technology is incorruptible. This system checks automatically for any recent updates and then makes any updates readily available to all active users on the network. A reconciliation of all transactions is also readily available. The network routinely updates its records once every 10 or so minutes.

This means that transactions are almost in real time.

The transparent nature of this technology is also admirable. Once data is uploaded and transmitted, it becomes readily available to the entire network publicly. You can always confirm through the blockchain if a transaction you entered has been processed. Unscrupulous people may try to corrupt this system, but it has proven over the years that it is incorruptible.

In fact, anyone attempting to make some changes or alterations to the block will require a lot of energy, something which most people cannot manage. It would also be a very costly process.

Blockchain as a network of nodes

As observed earlier, the blockchain consists of a network of computers, each of which is referred to as a node. A node is any computer that is connected to the blockchain network through a client. The client is one that can validate and relay any transactions within the network. Once transactions are updated, they are then relayed all across the network.

Chapter 5: The Blockchain

Within the network, each and every node has the capacity to act as a network administrator. Now, recall that the Bitcoin network is decentralized with no central command. Each joint within the network has an incentive to join in and so does this voluntarily.

The blockchain was developed just when Bitcoin was created. The main purpose of the blockchain is to support Bitcoin operations and keep it secure. As of today, however, this powerful system finds applications in many other fields.

Blockchain decentralized

Any operation that occurs within the blockchain does so as a function of the entire network. There is no central command where matters have to be approved. This concept makes it a very versatile platform such that it easily finds application in many other fields.

Other applications of the blockchain

One such field is the stock exchange. In such a field, the blockchain can be used to provide real-time data on all trades, providing a lot of openness and access to information that investors demand. Investors will not have to wait for days to receive information from their brokers but can find out almost instantly when their trades are processed.

There are many other members of the financial services community, such as banks and other lenders, who are seriously considering use of the blockchain as part of their operations. There are already blockchain software programs in use in some institutions, helping provide the versatility, openness, and security of this technology.

The enhanced security of blockchain

Most of the current systems in use today have many centralized operations. If data, for example, is stored in a server or other database, then it is highly prone to hacking. It is not lost on most consumers on how data they provide to organizations, both private and public, has been compromised in the past.

Hackers can access these centralized systems, steal the data or make other unauthorized use. This compromises the information, puts the customers at risk and some even lose their investments.

These challenges are eliminated through the use of the blockchain. Unlike most systems that make use of a username or password for accessing the centralized database, the situation is not the same with blockchain. All information is encrypted which adds an incorruptible layer of security to all transactions. Compromising such a system becomes almost impossible.

Blockchain is a level two network system

Anyone who trades or deals in Bitcoins has to have a computer connected to the Internet. The computer has to then get connected to the blockchain network. Now, in this case, the Internet is considered the level one network as it indirectly connects all users.

Within the level one network is the blockchain. It connects all users and is, therefore, a second level network. Both systems are decentralized and have no central command where all things are stored, managed and administered.

Last year, 2016, there were Bitcoin transactions on the blockchain worth about $200,000 daily. This is because the network allows users to interact directly with each other and transact. It shows that there is a very high level of security within this network.

Currently, firms such as Goldman Sachs are considering adopting this kind of network. A decentralized system such as blockchain will enable them to enhance their trades and speed up the clearance and settlement of trades. According to their estimates, this can save them about $6 billion every year.

Other applications of the blockchain

There are other possible and potential applications where the blockchain can definitely be used. One of these is the supply chain management. A lot of consumers all around the world want to know the true position of their goods and products in transit. This could be mail dispatched overseas, a packaged sent to a friend and so on.

Blockchain is designed such that it is able to provide real-time information to all clients so they can know what stage their products are. For instance, are they in transit, have they arrived and so on. The technology can come in very handy in this sector.

It can also be used in governance. The blockchain technology can ensure that there is openness in government operations and that the public can access any information that they are entitled to with little inconvenience. There are

Chapter 5: The Blockchain

platforms being designed that will ensure outcomes of elections and referendums and similar events are accessible to the public in real time.

Chapter 6:

Bitcoin Wallet

If you want to buy Bitcoins, then you must have a Bitcoin wallet. A Bitcoin wallet can be defined as a digital wallet where your Bitcoins are stores. In essence, however, a Bitcoin wallet is a software program that stores your Bitcoins but in the form of a private key. This private key occurs in the form of a string of numbers. These are supposed to be secret to keep from getting compromised.

The Bitcoin wallet is essential if you will receive and send Bitcoins. It is something you need to have. If you own a wallet, then you will receive ownership of the Bitcoin balance in your wallet.

Bitcoin wallet formats

Bitcoin wallets come in many different formats. These formats are in the form of desktop wallets,

Bitcoin

mobile wallets, hardware format and even a web-based wallet. At the moment, these four are the most popular.

The desktop wallet is the most secure and provides you with total control. Since it is offline, you can be guaranteed that it cannot be compromised. It is, in fact, advisable to ensure you have an offline wallet so as to keep all your Bitcoins safe from theft.

The digital wallet

In order to buy Bitcoins, you need to have a digital wallet. You need to ensure that you get a reliable and secure wallet because security of your wallet is absolutely important. Just as Bitcoins are an equivalent of real cash, the digital wallet is the equivalent of a real wallet. They perform the same function of keeping your currency safe.

In your digital wallet, you will store or keep your Bitcoins but you will use a secure private key to do this. This key is the one that allows you to access and sell or trade with your Bitcoins.

Web wallet: The web wallet allows you to access your Bitcoins from anywhere in the world and transact regardless of where you are located.

Chapter 6: Bitcoin Wallet

Desktop wallets can be offline. They are installed on desktop computers and allow users to have entire control. You can store your private key in this wallet and even create a Bitcoin address that allows you to send and receive Bitcoins.

A mobile wallet functions similarly to a desktop wallet only that it is now on your mobile phone. This makes it a very portable digital wallet that you can carry with you and even spend Bitcoins on the go.

Hardware wallets: Hardware wallets are not readily available but provide an alternative option for those who desire to have flexible or mobile Bitcoin wallets.

It is very important that you keep your Bitcoin wallet safe. The safeguards that are essential include use of a very strong password with alpha-numeric characters as well as using a cold storage option. This means storing the wallet offline. This way, no hacker will ever get to it and your Bitcoins will be safe all the while.

How to open your first Bitcoin wallet

If you want to deal in, invest in, or buy Bitcoins then you will need to have a Bitcoin wallet. It is through this digital wallet that you will receive

Bitcoin

Bitcoins, send Bitcoins and transact anytime you wish.

The Bitcoin wallet is simply an app or program. You can open one with the different Bitcoin firms online. Most people visit a trusted exchange or Bitcoin firms like CoinBase to open a wallet.

You can visit websites such as Bitcoin exchanges and Bitcoin organizations and then follow the steps provided to open your own wallet. The process is quite simple and involves filling in a form and providing some personal information. The details needed are quite minimal and will not compromise your security online.

It takes about 1 or 2 minutes to open a digital wallet. You will need to provide an email address because it is an essential communications tool. Once the process is complete, the wallet will be ready and you will be able to access it and start buying Bitcoins.

When buying Bitcoins, you can use regular currency such as dollars or pounds to buy at the exchange. It is much cheaper to buy at an exchange compared to other Bitcoin firms. On the blockchain, you can buy directly from another user. This way, you will incur no

Chapter 6: Bitcoin Wallet

additional costs other than the cost of the Bitcoins.

You do not have to buy your Bitcoins where you got your digital wallet. There is no requirement and so you should feel free to buy your Bitcoins anywhere you wish and open a Bitcoin account where you prefer. All you need to ensure is that the Bitcoin firm you deal with is reliable, trustworthy and credible.

The same applies when you want to buy Bitcoins at the exchange. You must make sure that you deal only with reliable sellers so that you do not lose your money. While most of the people dealing in Bitcoins are honest and decent people, always be cautious. It is better to wait a while longer before you buy Bitcoins, rather than buy then be disappointed.

At a Bitcoin exchange, you will come across many different Bitcoin dealers. They will have very attractive offers on their profiles. Therefore, search for sellers very carefully. Ensure that you deal with reputable dealers because some may not be very reputable.

Many exchanges will provide a rating system so that buyers can rate sellers and provide information about their experience. If a seller has great ratings, then they are probably worth interacting with. Many reputable sellers would not be ready to tarnish their names and will, therefore, be willing to ensure that deal fairly and openly with you.

If you can, always ensure that you keep your wallet offline and keep it safe. Ensure that you do not expose your Bitcoins to any unnecessary risks. If you keep them safe and follow the safety instructions and advice, then you will be able to keep your Bitcoins safe and you will be able to trade, buy, sell and even invest your Bitcoins.

Conclusion

Thank for making it through to the end of this book, let's hope it was informative and able to provide you with all of the tools you need to achieve your goals whatever they may be.

The next step is to find a trustworthy partner that can guide you in buying, selling and investing in Bitcoins. There are many firms online that deal in Bitcoins. There are also renowned institutions and even individuals who can advise you on how best to invest in Bitcoins.

Even as you get into the world of Bitcoins, you should take precautions and start slowly. Take small steps and tread cautiously. Investing in Bitcoins can be very rewarding but it also remains a risky affair. The risk in Bitcoins stems mostly from its volatile nature. Many investors buy and sell shortly thereafter, enhancing this risk.

Also, know that you stand to lose your money if things do not work out well. Any investment is risky and more so Bitcoin. Therefore, always make calculated risks and make sure you only use money that you can afford to lose. Also, it is better to buy and hold for some time. You stand to make more or better returns this way.

Finally, you may want to read further on Bitcoins or consult with an authority on this matter because, as much as the information provided here is detailed, it is by no means exhaustive. Further reading will only enhance your knowledge and further, confirm what you already learned from this book.

Finally, if you found this book useful in any way, a review on Amazon is always appreciated!

www.ingramcontent.com/pod-product-compliance
Lightning Source LLC
Chambersburg PA
CBHW050016230526
45470CB00003B/1000